This Too Shall Pass

Samantha Shafto

Presentation by *BookLeaf Publishing*

Web: www.bookleafpub.com

E-mail: info@bookleafpub.com

ISBN: 978-93-95890-64-9

First edition 2022

Forgiveness

Forgiveness is not weakness;
It allows the soul to heal
What you said in stress;
My mind and body thought was real

Forgiveness releases the pain you caused
me;
You have to forgive yourself to move
forward
My mind and body run free;
Can you trust your own word?

Forgiveness is who I am;
Also keeping my self-respect first
That's how I know I can pass God's exam;
You keep this up, you might be cursed

Forgiveness is how I walk lighter;
Proving to God every day, I am a fighter

Payton

I know I shouldn't blame myself,
As you left this world so abruptly
I loved you so much & had to put it on the
shelf
All of this is unjustly

Why did the world take my baby away?
What could have I done?
When all I wanted was for you to stay.
My Son.

Everything happens for a reason,
I'll never grasp that phrase
To them it will be over in a season,
To me this will go on for days...

I'll remind myself, It's not healthy to live here
and remember "This too shall pass", when I get
sad
I know you are always near

But that doesn't mean I won't, sometimes, be
mad

I will never know why they took you my
dear,
But, I know you don't want me to live in
fear...

Broken

This too shall pass,
Something that should be told to the mass
No matter what the feeling is,
Feelings left inside will start bubbling up like
fizz,
"This too shall pass" will not make you feel
like shattered glass

Oxford Strong

I was class of 2005
Walk around with my Wildcat Pride,
Never did I think this day would arrive
Nor how I would feel inside

Felt so hopeless, so far away
Blue & Gold run through my veins,
You shocked my town, you better pay...
My town was hurt, I felt the pains

Once a Wildcat, Always a Wildcat
We say with cheer
I'm sorry you're a child that
thought Oxford would go down in fear

We are Oxford Strong;
This is where we will always belong!

Anxiety

Persistent worry
Leaving your vision a little blurry
A disease for over-thinkers
also known as late night drinkers

Try and put it in the past
LOL let's see how long that might last
I can't sleep, do Penguins have knees?
How do you put the holes in Swiss Cheese?

They could be telling the truth, gut says it's
lies
There's a big surprise!
I wish I can walk around with pure pride
Instead of not knowing what to decide

Curse you Anxiety!
How do we fix this in this society?

The Hidden Truth

Family forgiveness
That can be a mess
Not letting you back is a vibe
It's completely okay to unsubscribe

I will always remember what was real
However, it's time for me to heal
The things I know you did
To let you back, I have to forbid

I can't see past the truth
You can lie, but I have proof
I will remember the love, laughs and things
Now, I get to grieve my wings

You were always there to help me around,
I'm sorry now I can't see past the clown

Lessons Learned

Thank those from your past
Even if the relationship didn't last
They were a lesson too
Now you have a new view
You'll eventually get the right cast

My Apologies

The window was unlocked;
Doesn't mean he had a right to come in
I stayed silent. I stayed shocked!
He beat you down, more than just your skin

I'm sorry I didn't protect you better,
I let you stand in the rain
When I should've protected you from the
weather,
I am not sure what was going on in my
brain.

I wasn't that busy,
Why didn't I let you grieve
Spent six years just dizzy,
I was the love you needed to receive

No one believed you,
I was there and saw the whole thing

Not sure why you needed anyone else's
view,
Especially from those that only saw you as a
fling

I saw it right there in front of your eyes,
But he said it was nothing...
And, I knew it was a disguise.
I'm sorry I sat there blushing

In your mind, crazy thoughts hosting
What did you ever do?
Really...Ghosting?!?
I finally let you speak and see the new

I'm sorry I didn't treat you better,
That strong voice went silent
Which only upset her,
No worries girl, I grabbed the wheel &
became the pilot

As I look into the mirror
I see the women I let down,

I've never seen her so clearer
She stands taller, with her feet firm on the
ground

She conquers, who conquers herself
I say with pride, about myself

Love

I am NOT hard to love
My independence fits me like a glove,
I know my worth plus tax
I love hard, a little stubborn, speak my mind,
these are all facts
Can you support me? Stand by my side? Lift
me above...

Raising the bar

Let me start with Thank-You
You know who
You raised the bar for me
You saw it, before I could see
I have the confidence of someone to pursue

11:11 makes me smile
I feel like that one is going to stay for awhile
Which also, helped me get to the next
phase
You have helped me in so many ways
Like it's not normal to feel like you're always
on trial

When I had a rough week, I get breakfast in
bed
Scared of the next move, then the amazing
things you said
I wake up to a Good- Morning text
I hate how I get perplexed
But, I get excited to see what's next

I love that I'm the independent, goofy me
Thank you for helping me see
I understand God didn't make me twice,
& It's okay that he did add extra spice
I know I'm more than a second choice
Basically, thanks for helping me find my voice

POV: Single Parent

Dating as a single parent
Let me be transparent
We don't have time for games
Our life has already been up in flames

Juggling a career & a life
Wondering how will we ever be the perfect
husband or wife
Picked ourselves up off the floor
Found something besides our kids worth living
for

Protecting our kids is full-time
Stop looking at us like that's a crime
Guarding our heart
Ready for the second phase to start

Please put your games away;
we've been through enough & ready for a new
day

I Don't Hate You

I wish you can feel what you put me through
Maybe you already do
However, I'm in love with the man you could
be
Have this feeling we'll never be a "we"
The love was so strong, but I don't hate you

At one point you were exactly what I
needed
For that I will never feel cheated
I don't hate you
I have the strength to let go and start new
I'll come back a brand new me, who will
never be defeated

My Name

If you decide to drag my name through the mud
Just remember my name comes from blood
I've worked hard to be the leader that I am
Not to, just do your job and say "Yes, Ma'am"

Clean past, the worst maybe a speeding ticket
I safely live on the edge, like the loop called Picot
Worked hard to be the best Mom I can be
Worked while pregnant to get my degree

Get knocked down twice, and get up three
That quote was written after me,
When you learn to control how you respond to it
That feeling my friend is lit

The truth is you have to live with the lies you
spread,
What's sad is you think that's how you will get
ahead!

Starting Over

I hit the floor
I know I'm about to go to war
No one in sight, but I'm feeling smothered
The world can see my life, nothing is
covered

How have I failed something else again?
Can I do anything right? Can't remember
when...
Career, relationship, life -
All feels like I got stabbed in the back with
a knife

I gave you every piece of me
Unfortunately, I can't say "we"
I feel so defeated
Will I ever feel completed?

I don't want to be stuck here
At the bar chugging a beer.
Hiding from issues
Or buried in tissues...
I've been knocked down before
I will NOT get used to this floor.

I just need to get passed day one
That's the start of my homerun

Go back to mass
Hear; This too shall pass...
Get out that blank page
Release me from this rage

Putting myself back together
I won't come down with the weather
I know my worth plus tax
I'm not falling through the cracks

Focusing on the past
Beginning the re-cast
Starting over
The beginning of closure

'vincit qui se vincit' tattooed on my chest
She conquers, who conquers herself is
clearly expressed
I am free
This is the new me

The Support Group

They start by picking up the pieces off the
floor
Show you signs you shouldn't ignore
Some stay and show true friendship
Some are lessons then dip
No matter what,they help you see what you've
never seen before

Success

Not married by 23

Can't figure out what you want for a degree

Don't drive a Ferrari

Don't feel sorry

Success is not about things, it's about being

happy and free

Watching The Storm

Lighting filled the sky
Anxiety melts away,
Not sure why...
Wish this feeling would stay

My safe space
Outside watching the storm,
Cuddled up next to a familiar face
Who knew later the bond that would form

I will make an oath
Come sit with me and watch the storm,
Later in life, this will bring growth
Tradition my Mom started, makes your heart warm

I love you to the moon and back,
Let's keep this tradition on track

I Don't Know Who Needs To Hear This

Don't bleed on someone who didn't cut you,
Heal first and be proud you grew.
Worry doesn't take away the troubles,
Nor does it help fix any struggles.

You did nothing wrong,
When you said that, you wanted to feel like
you belong.
Don't give up on you,
You're worth the fight, you can see this
through.

Stop playing games,
No need to put all their hearts through
flames.
You can miss them and still choose peace,
Let all those feelings release.

When you say, " I wish you the best" after
they broke your heart,
They lost the best thing for them, but now
you can restart.

Sometimes it doesn't work out because
they're a piece of shit,
This is a sign you need to stay split.
Casinos need a Phase 10 and a Uno table,
Although, I would not be able to keep my
savings stable.

When your boss is dick,
You can start over, but you should leave
quick.
When you find yourself eating ice cream on
the kitchen floor,
You are that much closer to the next open
door.

Be a decent human being,
That's one less car we will be keying.
You are enough,
It's okay that life is sometimes tough.

But, I'll be over here praying,
That you finally get the, "This Too Shall
Pass" saying.

Love being weird with you

I love how everything is new,
This all started because of you.
We may not be able to mop,
But our love is nonstop.

Crazy we found someone else who quotes
Twister,
Crazier you can give me #goosies with just a
whisper.
Searching for your hand,
Damn baby, that's in high demand.

Post-It's fill our walls,
Love reading all the recalls.
They can write a book on us,
Give the world a lot to discuss.

I gave up on lyrics long ago,
Now all of our feelings are pouring out of
the stereo.
Hope the 'Soulintioveibe' never escapes,
Gotta love those Cotton Candy Grapes.

I love that you think of me when you hear,
'You Make It Easy'
I can't get over how easy it is to be this
incredibly Cheesy.
Starting a blended family, Amen!
#838710

Hunter

Most Unique, voted by your class
That can honestly be seen by the mass
It's amazing watching you grow
Just remember it's okay to make mistakes, just let
life flow
I love you so much, even with all the sass

This Too Shall Pass

Whatever you're are going through,
You need to pursue
Sometimes the world is just an ass
But, this too shall pass...

You're no longer with someone you cared
about,
I promise you can live without
But, this too shall pass
I know this might sound crass

Everything is falling in place
Get ready for the disgrace
This too shall pass my friend
This will never end

Hurt and disgusted;
Feel used and distrusted
Depressed and Sad
Angry or Mad

Got Fired or Promoted
Prom Queen or Outvoted
Approved or denied for a loan
Either way this is how you've grown

Loss of a loved one,
It's okay to be sad, but don't be done,
Feel like you keep getting knocked over,
Get up, don't forget you're your own four-leaf
clover

Although it's okay, don't stay in the dark
Take the lesson, be stronger and leave your
mark
Because, what have I been teaching in
class?
This Too Shall Pass